THE CREATION
of the
WORLD

(Gwryans an Bys)

translated from the Cornish

by

Donald R. Rawe

Lodenek Press
Padstow,
Cornwall

ISBN 0 902899 74 0 (Hard Cover)

ISBN 0 902899 75 9 (Paperback)

Typeset and printed in Great Britain
by Lodenek Press

CONTENTS

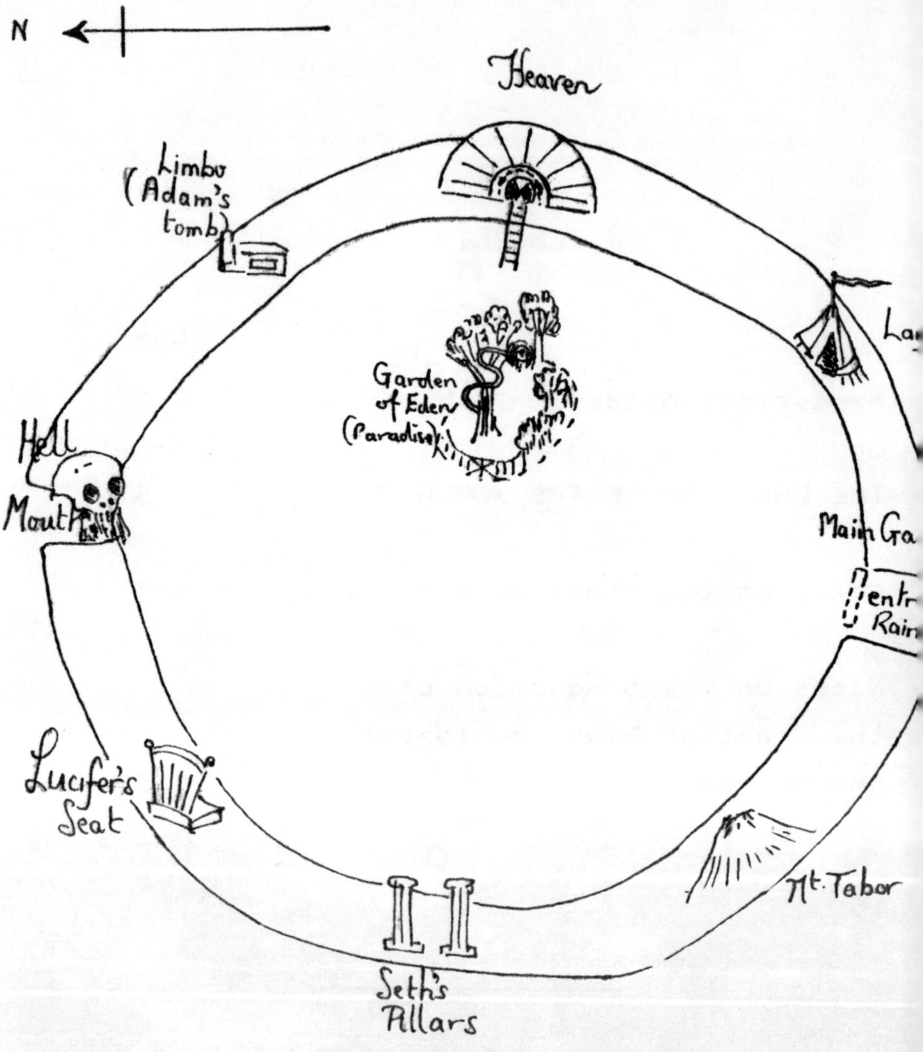

Piran Round

Stations adopted for 1973 production

THE CREATION OF THE WORLD

Historical Notes.

Gwryans an Bys, The Creation of the World, is the last of the three great Cornish biblical dramas we possess: the others being the 14th century cycle known as the Ordinalia (comprising the Origo Mundi, Passio Christi, and Resurrectio Domini); and the Camborne saint's play, Bewnans Meriasek (probably 15th century).

Gwryans an Bys was transcribed in 1611 by William Jordan of Helston, though it appears likely that the version he recorded dates from around 1540. The Celtic scholar, Dr. Whitley Stokes, who published the play with a literal English translation in 1864, considered that because of the reference to Limbo (whence the soul of Adam is consigned) parts of the play originate from pre-Reformation times. This sort of feature evidently lingered on, Cornwall being sufficiently removed from English ecclesiastical influence for it to be retained in vernacular performances.

John Keigwin of Mousehole again transcribed the play later in the 17th century; it was from his manuscripts that Stokes worked, though Davis Gilbert had published an unsatisfactory and inaccurate version in 1827. The Creation play has long fascinated many people, including students of the Cornish language and of drama itself. It represents the final flowering of religious drama in Cornish, and we can only regret that the second and third days of the play, dealing with the themes of the Passion and Resurrection, have not survived. (Here, perhaps, one should point out that there is literally no evidence that they were ever composed or performed. It is therefore possible, though unlikely, that they did not exist.)

Dramatically the material differs considerably from the Origo Mundi. It actually covers less ground, but in distinctly greater depth and sophistication. The Temptation episode presents greater complexity of thought and character; the Cain and Abel sequence is dramatically more effective than in the earlier play; and Noah's Flood is certainly more humorous and shows considerable development of character parts. But the greatest difference is that the Creation introduces perhaps the most impressive feature of all Cornish drama, making total use of the Cornish Round or plain-an-gwarry: the Fall of Lucifer and the Battle of the Angels. Dramatically, this idea is a masterstroke, and provides a spectacle unrivalled by anything in English mystery play cycles.

One feels that as recorded by Jordan, late 16th century Cornish drama was moving forward in pace with contemporary humanist thought. An instance of this is Cain's protest at the wastefulness of his sacrifice: not mere disobedience, but a reasoned revolt which any conservationist today will understand. Indeed the whole theme of the Creation play can be seen as man's awakening of his own powers, and the difficulties experienced by God the Father in keeping his new creature in his place.

Unfortunately for Cornish drama the Cornish

language itself was being fast eroded by the time Jordan wrote down this play, and puritanical movements within the church plus ill-founded disparagements of such local 'rustic' customs (vide the scornful remarks of Richard Carew on the plays) also contributed to the decline. Thus no one thought it worth translating the plays into English, though up to about 1620 during Corpus Christi week, they were certainly very popular. Dr. Neville Denny of Bristol University, director of the Ordinalia production of 1969, wrote: 'These occasions must have filled a place in the lives of 15th century Cornishmen approached only in modern terms by Christmas, football, pop entertainment, the circus, television, pantomime and spectacular pageantry. These Cycles were ...an art form triumphantly of the people and for the people, having something of moment to say to everyone. Though blunt and vigorous, they are a high water mark in the history of British drama, the most truly popular drama we have ever had.'

And enormously popular, seizing the public imagination, was Denny's Ordinalia, at Piran Round near Perranporth in 1969: re-opening, for an all-too-short space of five years, one of the traditional open-air amphitheatres of Cornwall for our native drama. Gwryans an Bys itself was revived in 1973 with the support of Cornwall County and other councils and benefactors. It was brilliantly directed by G. W. Finch, then Assistant County Drama Advisor. The present translation is a revision and refinement of the text used during those ten performances, heard and seen by some 2,000 people. The production was an unforgettable event for lovers of Cornish drama, and it is to be hoped that future performances will in time take place: for here surely is something unique which Cornwall can give the world.

In 1960 the Federation of Old Cornwall Societies published a version (in Unified Cornish spelling) of Gwryan an Bys, which was the work of R. Morton Nance (the Grand Bard Mordon) and A.S.D. Smith (Caradar). This was the basis of my present translation into modern, dramatically-usable English. I am, however, indebted to Mr. E.G. Retallack Hooper (former Grand Bard Talek) for many useful observations and suggestions. I hope that this modern version will be of service not only to drama students, but also to learners of Kernewek also. The Mordon-Caradar version is shortly to be republished by the Cornish Language Board, and a comparison of the literal English translation and this more colloquial one should be of interest to those engaged on the detective work of elucidating the finer points of the Cornish itself.

D.R.R.

THE CREATION OF THE WORLD

Music. Mist obscures all. God the Father appears and speaks through a cloud, moving as he does so.

THE FATHER

I am Alpha and Omega,
with neither beginning nor end:
here within the clouds, moving surely
over the face of the waters -
three Persons in one Godhead,
together reigning forever
in great honour and power.
Myself, my Son and Holy Spirit,
are three of one substance,
comprehended in one God alone.

The mist begins to clear.

I am God the Father,
all-powerful over everything there is.
Instantly now, by my grace, shall be created
Heaven - a noble place for mine own dwelling.
'Tis my will that it shall be my throne;
and there shall be made below it Earth,
at once complete in itself:

that shall henceforth be my footstool
for my honour and pleasure at all times.

<u>Music. Heaven is revealed: God ascends to it.</u>

Lo, Heaven is now created for me here,
exactly as I have devised and planned.
In it shall be placed creatures
to worship me continually with joyful song:
nine orders of glorious angels,
royal and splendid; my envoys
who will serve me always, as I have willed.

<u>The angels appear in turn, as called; they cross the arena and take up their thrones.</u>

I now ordain that each order
be seated on its throne:
according to their various degrees, each
one
shall be at my service as I command.
Here, next to mine own throne
shall the first three be created.
Cherubim, thou shalt be the highest:
Now come forth with all speed,
ye Seraphim and also Thrones.

Here shall ye worship me at all times,
as is my eternal will.
Thou, Lucifer, the Brightest -
for such is thy name - above all other
angels
shall thou sit, since thou art of the
first order.
Be sure to worship me, always at my side
as it behovest thou to do.

<u>Lucifer makes obeisance and takes up his place beside God.</u>

Now verily I say shall be made
in the second degree, three more orders:
come forth to me now, Principalities;
ye shall take your places here.
Powers to sit on this hand,
Dominions on the other.
Ye shall all praise and laud
My name for evermore.

<u>Choral music is heard as the orders assemble in Heaven.</u>

I will create below this
three further orders in the third degree:

Archangels,a very great order, come ye forth
to me here; now likewise Virtues;
and verily Angels shall sit here on the
right hand.
Ye shall all be missionaries for me,
performing my every behest
with greatest joy, and singing evermore.

Music swells, then fades out.

Since Heaven and Earth are created for me
now, according to my will
now that the nine great orders are
established,
now that the First Day has prospered,
I will hallow them by the words of my
mouth.

Music. He blesses Heaven and Earth.

I will descend to the earth beneath the
clouds
and there shall work my will:
so that I shall verily be seen
to be God without equal.

He descends to the plain.

Now on the Second Day
I shall forthwith create magnificence.
I will that light be made
in the sky above, and also
that the day be divided from the night.
By my almighty power
I shall have complete control
over everything upon the earth.
The ocean shall be drawn about
my land, to cleanse and wash it
constantly, at all times hence.

<u>Sound effects; sea noises.</u>

On the Third Day I shall cause
the trees to rise up, bearing
leaves both beautiful and good,
and surely also sweet flowers to behold.

<u>Trees and flowers appear.</u>

It is my will, that they shall bear
fruits of my desire, to nourish
all life hereafter.
On the Fourth Day the sun and moon
shall be created, and the stars likewise,
giving light for evermore.

Yea, all these are finely wrought indeed:
my blessing on them I bestow.

Music. Sun, Moon and Stars appear and perform a stately dance.

On the Fifth Day I am minded
to create, for my pleasure, fishes and birds,
and likewise all the beasts that walk the world;
and every sort of creeping thing.

Animals, birds and insects appear.

Behold: these are all most beautifully fashioned:
Truly I bless them, every one together.

Dance music. The animals, etc. parade around God, who blesses them, and then in a joyous act dances with them.
But the MUSIC CHANGES TO THUNDEROUS MENACE as Lucifer rises in Heaven.

LUCIFER

Peace! I say, all ye angels of heaven
Give me your attention now!

Am I not a mighty prince,
and the chief among ye, great and small?
Ye know my name: 'tis Lucifer,
a royal prince here in heaven,
equalled only by a few.
Ye also know I am greater than the
Father;
indeed, I am the Light of Heaven, no less,
like fire illuminating all,
more splendidly than the Trinity itself.
Bear witness, all, to this: that I
am a prince right glorious,
shining in golden splendour evermore,
without doubt brighter than the sun above,
as ye may all see.
I intend that no angel but myself
shall attain such a state as this:
I say I am as great as God himself,
and now command ye all on every side
to worship me in heaven.

<u>The angels murmur and confer among themselves.</u>

LUCIFER

Angels - ye have all heard me!
What say ye to me now?

Am I not a fine fellow indeed?
Answer me, every one:
for surely you know me by now.
The Father has gone forth from here:
I intend that he shall never come again
to heaven, if it lies in my power.

ANGEL OF LUCIFER IN 2ND DEGREE (BEELZEBUB)

Lucifer, I believe that thou art he
who eclipses all else in heaven.
Thou art created noble
and most powerful by nature;
therefore I will surely honour thee
above the Trinity itself.

Beelzebub descends to the plain and falls on his knees in obeisance.

ANGEL OF GOD IN 1ST DEGREE (MICHAEL)

O thou creature most unnatural,
to speak so against thy Maker!
Dost thou not remember thou wert made
in this very place by God, thou upstart?
Since thou dar'st compare thyself with Him,

thou shalt be greatly censured
and surely punished for it.

ANGEL OF LUCIFER IN 2ND DEGREE (TORPEN)

Who is this who dares to speak
so boldly against great Lucifer?
He has told ye all that his peer
does not exist in heaven,
and I believe that.
Behold him shining forth
more splendid than the sun itself.

(He descends and kneels to Lucifer)

Therefore I will honour thee, as I
ought to do.

ANGEL OF GOD, 2ND DEGREE

Be silent! - speak not so -
I pray thee, believe me when I say
that he who created him here
will destroy him again
whenever he wishes to.
If ye all persist in that belief,
ye will be sorry for it, be sure.

ANGEL OF LUCIFER, 3RD DEGREE

Whoever says that Lucifer the bright
is not worthy to govern us here
and be chief of all in heaven,
speaks lies, I say:
for he is worthy to be seated
on the throne like God forever,
and like God, he is without equal.
I will worship him properly, on my knees,
since he is so worthy to be loved.

Descends and kneels to Lucifer.

LUCIFER (from his own throne)

Inasmuch as I reign here
on my throne above all in glory,
all ye who hearken to me
shall sit here together
right by my side, I say.
I was made of thought:
ye should be pleased with such a person,
for in the noble estate of heaven
I am seemly in the sight of all.
Come up to me now, everyone:
I shall attempt to master God's throne.

In the Arena the Angels of God take up positions opposing the Angels of Lucifer.

MICHAEL

Lucifer, thou art unnatural
towards thy Maker:
therefore fear greatly, lest thou dost
earn
his displeasure, being worthy of it.
Stop to consider: thou wert indeed
created here by his act.
With a word he can destroy thee,
thou accursed one.

LUCIFER

Michael, thou art presumptuous
in opposing me.
I do believe that thou wouldst
set thyself up against me now.
Fear not, I say, thou shalt not,
neither thou nor any of thy fellows:
Therefore, one and all, do ye
worship and trust in me.
Ye shall see me shining
brighter than the Father:
for believe me, so I am.

The Father appears in heaven above them.

THE FATHER

Ah, Lucifer, Lucifer,
thou wert all the light of heaven
and always greatly exalted by me
and set on high. Now thou art
greatly unnatural to set thyself against
me.
For thy pride thou shalt be thrown down
into everlasting torment:
thus shalt thou be humbled.
I am fully determined now to create
a man from earth and soil
to serve me, and to fill
the place in heaven which shall be
voided
now by thyself and thy henchmen.
I ordain that hell shall be created
for thee: I command it instantly.

Thunder, fire and smoke. Hell Mouth opens wide as the Father names it.

There thou shalt abide
and with thee, every one of the nine
orders

who took thy part.
Thou shalt remain there in torture
forever mourning and in sorrow,
without ransom, until the end.
Thus have I spoken.

LUCIFER

What, dost thou will that man,
made of loathsome slime
should have my place here,
unrivalled in heaven?
That would indeed be dreadful
for a creature made of clay
to enter this place of glory:
he is unworthy of that, I say.
No! It shall not be so:
Thus I answer thee.
I shall certainly keep my place
from him, and from Thee also:
thou shalt see me, rebounding here,
proud and powerful!
Half of the angels are with me,
and agree to uphold me, Sire,
despite Thee, as you shall see.
For weal or woe
I will not go:
I tell you so.

Believe me,
This will not be -
for I reckon myself superior
to all who have yet been created!

THE FATHER

Silence, accursed Lucifer,
full of pride as thou art!
for soon, believe me, yes believe me,
thou shalt go to torment
without redemption.
All thy splendour and beauty
shall turn into ugliness
and vile filth.
Now, Michael, prince of my chivalry
and ye angels of the nine orders:
down with this revolt of theirs -
down, I say, master and man,
to dwell in foulest hell!
There let them live in torment
and direst sorrow forever -
yea, surely ever after.

Battle music. The angels group to attack Lucifer and his angels, taking up swords and staves.

MICHAEL

Now let us go, nine orders together,
and drive Lucifer forthwith
out of heaven.

LUCIFER

You, serf - I'll put to you this question;
why should God condemn me,
shining and powerful as I am?

MICHAEL

Because thou art accursed
and overproud in your heart:
thus I shall prove to thee by reason.
Thou fool, why didst thou not consider
that thou wert made by God's hand,
and also exalted by him
above all the angels in heaven,
seated here on this throne?

Lucifer attempts to mount God's throne.

LUCIFER

Right on the throne I intend to sit,
and to stay there despite thee still.

I and my fellows will prove with our
swords
that I am more worthy at all times
than the Father.

GABRIEL

Upon them now, all you of heaven:
drive him down to Hell and darkness!
And you, his henchmen,
depart with him as well!
Strike now with your swords!

BATTLE MUSIC. The opposing armies fight for a long while; at last Lucifer and his company are expelled and driven screaming into hell, foully apparelled and changed into Devils. Fire burns around them.

LUCIFER (at the gates of Hell)

Woe, alas! The end of my pretences!
I am in such darkness,
unable to leave it -
cast down into the deep pit of hell,
chained up with fire burning all round me.
Yet though happiness be denied me,
there are many angels come down
to live with me here.

MUSIC OF SORROW AND DAMNATION. Angels moan around Lucifer in hell. The victorious Angels return to Heaven and rejoin God.

THE FATHER

Lucifer, that evil reptile, is gone
out of heaven into darkness,
and now I shall create in his stead,
a man in the valley of Ebron
to fill the place he left.
Since we are One and Three together,
Father and Son in Trinity,
I forthwith create thee, Man, from clay
in Our own image,
and breathe into thy body
a spirit that thou mayst live.
And when thou shalt lose thy life
thou shalt turn to earth again.

(He creates Adam)

Adam, rise up obediently
and turn to flesh and blood.
Remember, I make thee of earth,
resembling myself from head to foot.
Take authority over all
that is on land and in the sea.

Thou shalt live until thou art grey,
in order to bring forth children.
Now for love of thee I will create
   Paradise:
a place sweeter than any to live in:
behold, 'tis made for my delight.

<u>The Father puts Adam into Paradise, where flowers and trees and a fountain appear, with the Tree of Knowledge and the apple on it.</u>

See, plenteous flowers of every kind
abound in this place
and fruit on every tree,
growing in summer and winter alike.
Now I grant to thee stewardship
over all fruits, and leave for thy
   pleasure
every plant and seed.

<u>(Indicates Tree of Knowledge)</u>

Yet always beware, I tell thee,
of this particular tree:
I charge thee above everything
not to interfere with it:
this is the Tree of Knowledge

of good and evil.
If its fruit be tasted
thou shalt be damned for it,
and sentenced to death -
be mindful of that!

Music. God watches Adam wandering in the Garden.

'Tis a melancholy thing, for sure,
to see Adam all alone, without a mate.

(He comes to Adam)

Now sleep, thou, Adam.

(Adam lies down and sleeps)

I will draw out a rib from thy side
and from it I will make thee a wife.

Eve is created.

Now from one of thy ribs
I make a mate for thee:
thine own, to help thee always.

Eve rises up. Adam awakes, sees and admires her.

ADAM

O my good Lord:
she shall be called woman, Eve,
this creature made from my rib.
O blessed thou art for this!

Fishes and beasts appear.

THE FATHER

Behold, Adam, the fishes,
birds of the air and beasts
that live on land and sea.
Give them their names,
and they will come at thy command.
But do not oppress them in any way.

Music. Adam dances with the animals. He points to them in turn and gives them names.

ADAM

I name cow and bull.
Let every animal take each its name:
horse and mare and ass,
dog and cat and mouse,
and the various birds and snakes.

Geese and hens appear; also a fine serpent with a virgin's face and fair hair.

I give names to the fishes:
bream, gurnard and eel:
so I account them, one by one.

Music ceases; the dance ends.

THE FATHER

Since everything created in these six days
is wholly good and fair,
I will bless them:
thus the Seventh Day shall be sacred,
a Day of Rest, for all men
who shall be saved.
As a sign of that
I shall forthwith rest

The Father departs to heaven in a cloud. Hell fumes. Lucifer appears at its gates with other Devils.

LUCIFER

I have suffered a foul throw,
hurled out of heaven into the pit of hell.
Thus is my state ordered!

Now I am in direst torment,
lasting till the end of time.
There is no remedy for me:
so great was my transgression -
'tis useless to seek for mercy.
I know the Father will not forgive
my rashness,
Therefore I'll speedily wreak all the
  vengeance
I can think of, with great malice:
I care not who suffers!
I know that the Father has created
a man from clay,
his body made in His image,
all most seemly.
I cannot tolerate that!
I am envious of him
and will contrive a plot
to cheat him if I can.
He is appointed by God
to be steward of all Paradise:
I'm aggrieved to see him exalted
whilst I'm humiliated!
That same man has a wife,
a woman called Eve:
she was made out of his rib,

wondrously beautiful above all else -
but she has a fickle mind.
As I'm a crafty fellow, I'll find a way
to tempt her, if I can.
Now Adam: he's lording it
like a duke in Paradise
whilst I'm left standing in hell
in everlasting fire,
burning in scorching heat.
I know well enough that this Adam
is created to fill again the rooms
of heaven, left empty by me and my
fellows
because of my great pride.
But, if by some scheme
I could win Adam's trust,
I'd bring him to such torment
he'd never get to heaven!
Ah, if only he'd listen to me! ...
Well, I will try Eve:
she is surely easier to deceive
than Adam, being more foolish-minded.
But twill never do for me
to be seen in my own form.
Nothing could be more hideous,
so horribly defaced am I -

as you can all see.

BEELZEBUB

Yes, you're ugly enough, I'll swear:
there is nobody more hideous
among all the devils.
You must think of a scheme, or this
  business
won't be worth so much as an egg!
Eve will tremble at the very sight of you,
so frightful you are in this form.
If you can make a proper bargain
you'll be upheld, despite God,
all-wise though he may be;
if he's deceived by this
I shall be quits with him!

The serpent appears on the plain.

LUCIFER

Don't worry, I'll be one jump ahead of him,
and bring Adam to torture. I'll tell you
  how ...
Among the creatures in this world
the Father made, in his wisdom,
a reptile called Serpent, with a face

resembling a beautiful virgin.
'Tis more subtle than any beast
or creeping thing on earth.
I shall enter into that serpent
and get into Paradise secretly.
Since it cannot speak at all
I shall conduct it as I wish,
and work some mischief with both
Adam and Eve, when I get there.

TORPEN

Yes, do that I entreat you,
as you are a cunning demon.
If you succeed you will be
honoured forever, and
chief ruler over us, no mistake!

LUCIFER

You'll soon see:
I'll trick the serpent quickly enough,
despite her pretty face.

(Approaches the serpent; she avoids him)

Confound you -
Stop and be ruled by me!

Now let me enter in.

You needn't fear,

since you're so comely.

(He strokes and subdues her and enters into the serpent)

You'll certainly be accepted

and believed by Eve:

your countenance will please her.

Since I am so closely intertwined

with you, see, my voice

is all changed, like a maiden's.

My treachery won't be discovered;

I'm pretty clever, I reckon.

I'll travel without making a sound,

not even a rustle, real smoothly,

up into the tree, as fine as an angel!

Sinuous music. Lucifer, as the serpent, enters Paradise and climbs the Tree of Knowledge. Eve is walking in the Garden.

EVE

I will go for a walk in this place

among the flowers.

Look, here is every

pleasant thing in the world,
growing here, so comforting to me.

SERPENT

(sings a song of temptation up in the Tree)

Eve, why don't you come and talk,
come and talk to me?
Eve, I know what you would like,
you would like to see.
It would make me happy now,
happy now to know,
If you'd only trust to me,
trust to me, I vow.

Eve looks at the tree, wondering.

EVE

Who are you, up in the tree
singing and making these sounds?
I marvel to hear you,
and wonder where you come from,
because I have no business with you.

SERPENT

Don't be surprised, good woman.
I have come here from heaven

as fast as I could, to speak to you
quite privately.
I beg you above all, don't be amazed
or afraid at seeing me.

EVE

I'm not afraid, nor have the slightest
doubt,
since your face is so becoming:
For by what you say, it seems
you have just arrived from heaven:
and if you come from there,
you are indeed welcome to me,
and the more to be believed.
Tell me your errand, and if
I can help you, it won't be in vain.

SERPENT

My mission will be profitable
if you will trust me.
But I fear there will be great trouble
if you betray me.

EVE <u>(comes nearer to him)</u>

No - I won't betray you for anything, my
friend.

So if your errand seems good,
you can carry it out;
I'm sure 'tis very worthy.

SERPENT

Upon my word, good wife, fear no danger:
'tis good and seemly too.
Otherwise, if I should fail
'twould be a great sin,
and worthy of punishment.

EVE

You're right, good creature:
That would be terrible, indeed:
I'm longing to know your errand.
Tell me now, I pray.

SERPENT

I shall tell you, Eve;
listen to me very carefully.
You can be as wise as God on high,
and shall know everything.

EVE

By St. Michael! My thanks indeed;
I'd be so happy if

I could come to that!
'Twould be splendid to be close
to God above, equal in every way with him,
and held to be as wise.
Then truly, by the saints,
I could rule nobly,
and live in state as I wished!
I beg you, tell me how to do it:
I can't bear to wait any longer,
I shall surely suffer
Unless you tell me straightaway.
My woman's wit is weak
and I'm not very clever:
tell me this news right away -
Please, I pray you do!

SERPENT

I'll tell you, Eve. If you taste
the fruit here on this tree
you will become as wise
as God in his high heaven, above.
'Tis no lie I'm telling you.

Eve is angry and makes to go.

EVE

What? is that your trick?
your advice can't be trusted, and
I'll tell you why.
God has laid down to the contrary,
that we must not taste that,
and gave his strict commandment
that we must not interfere with it.
Why do you tempt me like this?

SERPENT

Listen, Eve, and come closer.
I am sorry to find
that you believe that story.
I'll tell you why
God gave you that order:
if you tasted this
you would be as wise in every way
as He himself.
The Father would not desire
anyone else to be so wise
as to know both good and evil.
And so, good Eve,
I won't deceive you
nor tell you lies.
Trust my advice
if you want to be exalted:

either you listen and agree,
or be like children for ever -
sweet Eve.

EVE

Yes, yes, I'm listening:
but He charged us so strictly
that we shall be punished and grieved
if we break one single jot
of his commandment. No doubt
we shall be cast into hell
to live there forever if we do not obey.

SERPENT

Hush, Eve; how foolish you are -
you won't trust good advice.
I assure you, you'll be sorry
if you reject it. I'm not pleased with you;
I wouldn't advise you to make
such a fine bargain, if I didn't love you.

<u>EVE (approaches the Serpent again)</u>

If only I knew this was true
I should do as you desire,
seeing you come from heaven.

SERPENT

That's true, good woman;
you needn't distrust me,
for only good people come from heaven;
and I'm one of them.

He lowers the apple for Eve to take.

Give part of it to your husband,
for this affair's worth nothing
unless he has his share.

EVE

I won't be so greedy as to keep
it all myself. Surely
I love Adam beyond everything -
God forbid I should keep his share from
him!

SERPENT

I will hold out the branch -
take the fruit from it.

EVE

Certainly, so I will.

I can't wait long -
I must taste it.

SERPENT

Never fear, you'll be happy indeed.
You'll see everything with your eyes wide open,
and become as wise as God, no doubt about it.
I tell you, Eve, I wouldn't have you
exalted so high for anything, unless I loved you.

EVE

Many thanks, kind sir, for your sound advice.
I'll trust you, and I'll taste the apple
right away, by Heaven.
My husband will be grateful to me
for taking part in such a venture -
by God the Father of the Trinity,
he'll set me up high
and praise me for this!

<u>She takes the apple and bites it.</u>

SERPENT

Away now, good Eve;
you'll thank me for this.
And that good man, Adam,
will make much of you.
You won't regret this bargain.

EVE

Farewell, my friend from heaven:
I shall love you always.
Now I'll put my best foot forward
to greet Adam, and give him the apple.

SERPENT

Do that, I beg you:
you'll hear more news before seeing me
again.

Eve goes to Adam and presents him with the apple.

EVE

Adam! Adam, where are you?
Listen to me, and come here.
I have something to please you -
I'm not playing tricks;
you'll thank me for this.

ADAM

Welcome, Eve, my good wife.
If this news is good you'll be rewarded
and shall have my heart always,
at your pleasure.

EVE (showing the apple to him)

Look - look at this:
see what a fine apple I have for you!
If you take a bite from it
'twill bring you more profit
than thousands of pounds.

ADAM

Come here, let me see whether
'tis a good apple. Tell me
where 'twas found.

Eve gives him the apple; he recoils.

EVE

What, are you afraid to look at it?
Adam, my husband - tell me, I pray.

ADAM

I don't like the look of it.
I fear 'tis no good: I believe
I shall be in trouble if this
was picked from the forbidden tree.

EVE

Don't worry about that,
Sweet Adam, my love.
If 'twill please you, I'll tell you
how I got it.
As I was wandering, I heard
up in the tree a sweet angel singing.
I was wondrously pleased
to see him in the tree;
in friendship he offered me
many worthy things, by my faith.

ADAM

Ah, Eve, Eve, you have done wrong
to listen to that angel!
I reckon 'twas an evil fellow
you heard singing, telling you
to pick that apple.

EVE

He spoke to me so winsomely, husband,

I couldn't refuse him anything.
And his promises were so tempting
they made me trust him.
Upon my soul, I never suspected any
   deception!
His offer, 'twas bounteous!
If we tasted that fruit
we should become as God,
as wise as Him, too.
It seemed to me then, if we could
come to that, 'twould indeed be
a fine bargain.

ADAM

O shame upon you, Eve!
I curse the thought!
We deserve the great misfortune
we are cast into!
'Twas a dreadful agreement, I tell you.
Precious little gain we'll get by it,
when you reckon it up, alas!

EVE

Hush, Adam don't be angry:
No harm has come of it yet.
I was afraid of the same thing,

and told him so, of every danger;
but he assured me, on his peril,
I had nothing to fear from this.

ADAM

O curse that villainous creature,
and you too along with him.
We'll certainly suffer for this affair of yours,
and deserve all the censure we get.

EVE *(angrily)*

Yes - oh yes, I'll get all the blame
from you, Adam - whichever way the game goes.
But if we became gods, would you be vexed?
Devil a bit, I know that, well enough.

ADAM

Hush, hush - please don't be foolish.
The serpent was too cunning for you this time:
He told you enough lies, and you believed them.

You'll see my words proved right -
there'll be great punishment for this.

EVE

O yes, you're the wise man:
you won't trust me! I tell you,
if I don't get what I desire
you won't see me a moment longer!

(She makes to go.)

'Twas an angel up in that tree;
he spoke plain words to me
and I believed them.
In other words, man,
taste that apple - or lose my love.

(She offers the apple)

Look - take this lovely apple,
for certain, the love between us, man and
wife,
will die if you don't eat it.

ADAM

This is a sorry state of things:
I have to listen, or lose the love

ordained between us!
Sweet Eve, don't be angry;
I'll do all you wish.
Let me have it, and I'll eat it now.

EVE (gives him the apple)

Yes, do it for me:
And as long as I live,
you will always have my love.
See, here's the apple:
take and eat it right away,
lest I get angry with you.

He takes the apple, bites it; then throws it away.

ADAM

O, O, misery! I have sinned,
and done what was forbidden!
O you wicked woman, without grace,
you've deceived me basely.

Eve looks upon Adam very strangely, and is speechless.

Look: our bodies are naked all over.

Let us cover our private parts up
with green leaves.

<u>They cover their members.</u>

Truly, I know that God the Father
will be very angry with us;
I'm sureof it.
Look, Look! - do you see him, Eve? He's
coming!
Let's go away for shame,
and hide on some secret place.

<u>They hide.</u>

<u>Music, heralding anger.</u>

THE FATHER

Adam, Adam, what art thou doing?
Why dost thou not come forth to welcome me?

ADAM

Because of my nakedness,
having no garment, I went away
from Thee, to hide in this place.

THE FATHER

Who hath shown thee that thou wast naked,
in feet, body or arm,
except that fruit, which thou
be not allowed to eat without sinning?
Why hast thou done so?

ADAM

Thou gavest me a wife:
she is to blame for it all.
'Twas she who picked a fine apple
and brought it for me to taste.

THE FATHER

Since thou didst listen to her
and acted despite my forbidding,
thou shalt work in thine own sweat,
labouring for food to the end of thy
days.
Eve: why didst thou deceive thy husband
without cause?

EVE

The serpent tempted me to do that,
by his treachery:

and he promised me
that we should always profit by it.
That is the truth.

THE FATHER

Since thou didst hearken to him
and deceived thy true mate,
I ordain woman to be
always subservient to man.
Mark my words well -
her travail shall increase
for disobeying my commandment;
Nor shall she ever bring forth a child
without great labour.

(To serpent)

O cursed one, tell me
why didst thou deceive them?

SERPENT

I'll tell thee how it was:
they had such great happiness
when I was burning all the time.

THE FATHER

Serpent, for tempting them
great punishment shall be ordained for
   thee;
cursed art thou beyond everything -
beyond any beast or reptile in this
   world.
Man shall forever have fear of thee;
and thou, reptile, shall creep
and slide at length on the ground.
Between her children and thee
I will create enmity for all time,
such as will surely grind thy head
into the ground.

LUCIFER (the Serpent)

This is a wretched state of things -
Well may I cry out and groan!
I've turned out to be a bungler:
so I'm awarded great punishment,
in the pit of hell, my own citadel.

Lucifer comes out of the serpent.

I must begin to creep and slither
on my belly along the ground.
See, I return to my own shape -

a great evil villain.
But though I can have no happiness,
that peasant, Adam, and his Eve,
will come to me in hell,
and their children too for ever;
as ordained by the Father's word.
Let the serpent stay there,
never to come out of that place;
for 'tis cursed indeed.

He creeps to hell on his belly, with great noise.

ADAM

O Father God in thy glory,
since I am cast into evil,
I pray thee, grant to thy creature,
a drop of the Oil of Mercy.

THE FATHER

Adam, before the world ends
I will grant to thee the Oil of Mercy,
and also to Eve thy wife.
But verily I tell thee
because thou didst listen to thy wife
and for picking the fruit I forbade thee
- I curse the ground -

It shall bear for me thorns and briars,
and you shall eat the herbs of that same
ground
for thy bread, in the sweat of thy labour,
until thou dost once more become
the same earth I first made.
From the dust here wast thou made:
back to dust shalt thou return.

Music. The Father ascends to heaven.

ADAM

O Lord of Heaven and earth as well,
may thy will be fulfilled.
Perhaps I shall be happy
before the world shall end,
and shall find the Oil of Mercy;
though punishment is waiting for us
in some place in hell -
we have surely deserved it
for breaking the Law.

THE FATHER (in heaven)

Michael, bright angel, descend
and with a sword of fire
drive Adam and his wife from Paradise;

but take to them two garments
to cover them at all seasons
so that their nakedness shall not be seen.

MICHAEL

Lord, I shall do that.
I have everything ready to go to them.

Michael descends with attendant Angels.

Adam, go out of this land,
to dwell amid the world:
thou thyself shalt dig,
and along with you your wife shall spin.

The angels give them garments of skins, and they depart from Paradise. Outside they put on the garments, and find a spindle and distaff.

MICHAEL

Here is clothing for you,
Adam and Eve. Hurry - put them on!
You cannot stay here:
make for the way out!
See, here are your tools to dig,
and your things for spinning, all ready.

Death appears, some way off.

DEATH

I am God's messenger, Death,
appointed by him here.
Because he broke the commandment
ordained for him by God,
Adam and his issue shall die.
So 'tis appointed for all
who live in the world,
that I should slay them with my dart.
If Adam and Eve had not sinned
and broken the Father's Law,
they would not taste death
but live for evermore in joy.
He was appointed here
chief warden over Paradise;
now through the sin of covetousness
all his joy is lost; and so
he will be punished for it.
They were deceived by the devil
through the accursed serpent,
as here you have all seen.

Death departs.

ADAM

This is a great calamity -
because of that evil serpent
we have been so foolish, and the place
ordained for us here to live in,
full of happiness forever, is lost to us.
O Eve, my own wife, 'twas your own folly,
and great pain awaits us for it,
and lamentation too.

EVE

So many fair words I heard
I did not know how to deal with him.
Upon my soul, I supposed
'twas an angel of heaven sent to me.
Good sir, even if I be hanged for it,
his flattery was so glorious
I didn't know what to do!

ADAM

Alas, that you believed
Lucifer and his evil talk.
He was too cunning for you
when he went into that serpent
to deceive you.
Now I am without shelter,

driven out of Paradise:
I'll start digging to get
nourishment and bread,
and clothing to wear
for myself and my children.

EVE

I also will spin, to make
clothes to cover me
and the children I have borne.

ADAM

O woe that I was born
for breaking God's command!
We are driven out of paradise
into the world, to our misery.
I find nothing here of any use
and nowhere any food, other than beasts.
How shall we keep ourselves alive?

EVE

There is no Paradise here,
not this place, Adam, far from it!
There were fair flowers and fruits
to nourish us there,
whenever we looked for them.

Now the order of things is changed.

'Twas woe to listen to that serpent!

MUSIC. They dig and spin. Time passes.
Abel and Cain appear.

ADAM (beckons to them)

Two sons are born to me:
they are grown to men now,
as you may all see.
My elder son is Cain,
and the younger is Abel:
good and obedient children.

(Speaks to them)

I will set you a task:
one for each of you,
to look after our corn and cattle.
Cain, your charge shall be
over oats, barley and wheat,
to render the proper tithe.
And for Abel, the sacrifice
of beasts and the oxen
and all the sheep of the field.
When we have to pay tithe
take them to Mount Tabor

and burn them there,
for fear of God's wrath upon you
if you do not make proper oblation.

CAIN

Adam, beloved father,
I'll discharge your command exactly,
without fail. 'Tis most necessary
to labour and till in this world
to get ourselves food.

ABEL

I will go to the mountain now
to render the tithe,
burning this lamb to ashes;
and a whole tenth part of everything
I shall deliver up by fire,
as sure and certain sacrifice.

CAIN

Hold your tongue, Abel, you thickhead.
I'll burn neither the corn nor the fruits;
I'll gather thorns and prickles
and dry dung that will burn, and no
matter:
'twill make a great mass of smoke.

Cain, this is no good.
Let us make our rightful sacrifice
in worship to God the Father.
He deserves to be glorified
with the best fruit at all times -
I'll do it, if I have to die.

(Lights his sacrifice)

Look, Cain, my brother - consider:
this is sweet smoke.

CAIN

You be hanged! Shut your mouth!

(Lights his sacrifice of thorns and dung)

This is better, you whining fool!

ABEL

How can it be better,
making your sacrifice with cow-dung?

CAIN

By God my creator,

I wish you were strung up high!'
You whoreson knave,
I'll knock you down on the back of your
   head
for going against me!

(Takes up a jawbone)

Take that, you filthy rascal,
right on the jaw
with a jawbone!

Strikes Abel with jawbone.

ABEL

O misery, woe!
Cain, my brother, you have slain me.
For your deed you shall suffer
certain retribution,
be sure of that!

He dies.

CAIN

Here's a miserable peasant - dead.
I won't be ordered about!

Well, I'm rid of him now -
if only he were hidden in some ditch!

<u>He drags the body into a ditch.</u>

This fellow wanted to burn our corn!
I couldn't bear that.
God has no need of our things,
I know that much.
My father may be angry
when he hears the news he's dead;
but I'm the heir - it won't worry me!
Look at him, slain by my hand,
thrown in the ditch to rot!
Not a regret in the world for me -
I'm a smart dealer, surely.

<u>Music. Heaven is revealed.</u>

THE FATHER

Cain, tell me, where is Abel?
Answer thou me straightaway.

CAIN

I don't know, Lord, truly:
surely you know that.

I'm not his keeper -
maybe a wolf killed him
some way off - (aside) the filthy
   whoreson!
he's old and experienced enough now -
if he can't look after himself
I won't be his servant.

THE FATHER

Lo, the voice of thy brother Abel's
   death
continually cries out from the ground
upon thee in every place.
May thou be cursed forever:
and all the land thou dost own,
be accursed for thy deed.
May it never bear wholesome fruit,
nor any other goodness ever!
My curse I lay upon thee -
the curse of my Son and Spirit
now take on thyself.

CAIN (afraid)

I hear thy voice, O Lord,
but Thy face I do not see,
to my sorrow.

My evil deeds and sins
are more than thy mercy can forgive.
Now I am weak and defenceless
more than anyone in the world:
I see no reason why
they should not all slay me
because of this same deed.

THE FATHER

It shall not be so, Cain:
For any man who kills thee
shall undergo seven deaths.

<u>He marks Cain's forehead with the word Omega.</u>

I make this sign upon thee:
when it is seen, you will never
be touched by anyone.

<u>Music. The Father departs to Heaven which closes.</u>

CAIN

I will go to my father
and see how he will take the news.

(He comes to Adam)

God prosper you, my father!
I have made a great sacrifice
and burnt much corn.

ADAM

'Twas well done indeed.
But where is Abel? Tell me -
What, has he not come?

CAIN

If you're worried on his account
ask his keeper about him.
Don't ask me - I'm his brother.
I reckon he's worse than a bucca:
I don't know where he's wandered off.

ADAM

'Tis a frivolous answer,
my heart is sick to hear this
from you now.
By my faith - you've killed him!
You shall surely have
my curse on you for this

and your mother's curse as well.
When she hears the news her heart will break.
Execrated one, get you gone
from here this instant!
I won't endure the sight of you!
I can't stand upright for very grief,
hearing your words; I fall to the ground
now, my heart broken in two!

CAIN

I'm reviled enough -
no need to curse any more.
I shan't bother you or my mother again -
remember that.
I'll go right away at once
and wander the land around.
The curses are so heavy
I doubt if I shall find a place to stay in.

Adam is prostrate on the ground; Eve comes to him, tries to raise him.

EVE

Adam, what is the matter
that you're so upset?
It grieves my heart surely

to find you in this state.

ADAM

O Eve, my dear wife,
my heart is almost broken;
all my joy is lost indeed
because the child we loved the most
is dead.

EVE

I can't understand your grief -
our two sons were alive and well,
thank God, a little while ago.
Don't be upset - surely you remember,
Cain and Abel are ordered to make an offering
on Mount Tabor. Look -
there is Cain, soon returned!
Stand up, I beg you -
away with misery: away -
I can't give you better advice than that.

ADAM

Eve, this deed cannot be hidden from sight.
Abel is slain. Bear up!

EVE

(cries out, tears her hair, falls down upon Adam. Calmana, Cain's wife, and his children enter, some way off)

What, Abel killed?
God forbid 'tis true!
There's no man in the world
to commit such a murder, except you -
and Cain, my elder son.

ADAM

By Cain the cursed
is my son Abel slain:
I am born to great tribulation.
The wrath of God increases
hour by hour, and all around.
As long as I live in this world
He willsurely punish me:
There will be no joy in anything at all.

EVE

Alas, alas; what can be done?
This is bitter news!
My heart is broken - I wish I were dead!
If only I had never been made!
O you, accursed Cain -
my malediction on you forever!

'Twas an evil deed you did;
both heaven and earth
will cry out upon you always.
From this day forth
we shall never rejoice,
but be forever mourning
for your evil act.
Therefore get gone
and never trouble us again:
you son of curses!
Both day and night forever
you shall have my curse
and your father's too!

CAIN (beckons to Calmana and children)

I shan't worry about that:
I say the same to you, mother.
I know I'll never prosper in this world
so I'll go away, I don't know where;
I'm off!
To hell with my sorrow
for killing that fellow Abel -
because I never loved him.

(To his wife)

Get my things together;

After this I'll go right away
to wander in the wilderness.

CALMANA

O Cain, Cain, my dear husband,
you have done a dreadful deed
by killing that good man Abel.
He was your own brother,
and mine as well;
'twas against nature
for you to go and kill him.
God's wrath is on us for it!

CAIN

Rubbish! Cat's fart on it!
I shan't repent of it, not yet.

ADAM (to Eve)

Cheer yourself, my wife:
give over weeping and wailing.
Let us thank our Maker
for our labour in this world:
we have deserved it and more.
From now on let's live together chastely,
and forswear entirely this world's carnal
pleasure,

with merciful God's consent.

Music. Heaven opens.

THE FATHER

No, Adam, thou shalt not live in that way.
Thy seed shall increase
until it be without number:
'tis so ordained.
Thou shalt have another son,
born of thy body; mistake not that.
He will be as like thee
as any man can be,
and I shall love him.

Adam kneels.

ADAM

Lord, blessed be thou
for warning me thus!
May thy will be fulfilled always.

Music. Heaven closes.

CAIN

Hurry, Calmana, my sister -

let us go off now.
'Tis high time we journeyed hence.
Bring with us our necessaries,
my wife and sister, daughter of mother and
father.
The wrath of the Father goes with me
for killing that bighead, Abel,
and I have my parent's curse as well,
a hundred-fold.

CALMANA

O Cain, you were very wrong
to do that same deed.
You are cursed for it.
Our father and mother
are in deep mourning;
they will never forgive this murder.
Their grief is so great
that their hearts are broken,
I dare swear that.

CAIN

I don't care a straw about it,
or for them either!
They've been angry enough with me,
and cursed me so much, I know

I'll never prosper in this world.
So let's get away from here, far away
from my father. I mean to dwell
in woods, or in bushes and brakes,
for I dare not be seen,
even if I die because of it.
The murder was so great
that God cannot forgive me:
I dare not even show
my face to the Father
to seek forgiveness.

(He shows the mark to her)

CALMANA

You've only yourself to blame for that:
God set his mark on you,
right here on your forehead,
and spoke these words:
whoever sees this and kills you
shall suffer seven-fold for it.

CAIN

I don't give an eggshell for that promise.
I shan't trust in that
for fear of being let down.

Now everything is ready.
Let us go, far away from here
and wander the world.

(They take up bundles)

And our children with us -
since they're so tiny
I'll take some on my back.
Quickly, now.

CALMANA

I pray you, do that:
I'll lead the girl by the hand.
My heart is vexed -
I never had so much affliction
since I was born.

They depart into the wilderness.

Hell smokes. The Devils crawl out and take Abel's body to Hell.

ADAM

Glory be to God the Father!
A son is born to me
and grown to a fine youth.

(Seth appears)

This son is called Seth:
here he is, as you see.
I pray to the true Trinity
that while he is on earth
he will be a faithful servant to Him.

Music. Heaven opens.

THE FATHER

Adam, I say to thee
that I have chosen thy son Seth
to serve me always.
He shall be filled with knowledge
and skill: there shall be no science
in the world or universe
he shall not know inside out.
By the sun and stars above
he shall discern everything
that shall be hereafter,
both good and evil.

Adam and Seth kneel before God.

ADAM

Great glory to thee, my Creator

and Maker of all the world.
Thou art Lord without peer;
be thou worshipped everywhere.
Whoever honours thee will not fare ill.
May your will be fulfilled
through Seth, at all times, in full.

SETH

I will also faithfully serve thee,
Lord of Heaven, as I must.
Since you are so mighty
hear my voice whilst I live
here in this world,
that I may have grace hereafter
to behold thee in bliss
with thine angels high in heaven above.

Music. Heaven closes.

INTERVAL

LAMECH (emerges from his tent)

Peace! all you that are hereabout,
listen to me.
My name is Lamech, and I am the son

of Methusaleh.
I am the seventh descendant of Cain,
son of Adam. I am considered
a great lord, without equal
among those living: they all honour me,
as they should.
I'm a pretty bad lot -
I don't do many good turns,
but rob the poor folk when I can:
that amuses me.
And though my forefather, Cain,
is said to be bad enough,
I shall take it as a slight
if I'm not found to be worse than him.
I have more than one wife
for my pleasure - in fact,
I'm the first man ever to have two wives.
Also I have plenty of girls -
they're not fastidious -
I find them as I want them.
Devil a single one I spare
if they're pretty.
But I'm strangely afflicted:
I can scarcely see at all.
On my soul, I don't know
what the devil's to be done, or
where to find help.

The one pleasure I have in this world
is shooting with the bow.
I'll go right now to the forest,
away to kill strange animals.
Until now, we have never tasted
the flesh of those beasts,
nor eaten meat at all,
nor do we take any wine:
we have other food
and means to live well enough.
I make clothes for myself
with the hides of those animals
like my forefathers did.
My ancestor Cain is still living
among the beasts in the wilderness:
cast into disgrace for angering
God the Father; an evil fellow,
heaped with curses.
Come here, my servant, and bring my bow.
I'll go to roam the bush
and spy out wild beasts,
to slay some of them with my arrows.

SERVANT

Here are your bow and arrows, all ready:
I'll guide you into the woods
where you'll find plenty, for sure.

<u>Servant leads Lamech into the forest.</u>

CAIN <u>(in the bush)</u>

I am forgotten by everyone:
few people even know about me.
I am Cain, elder son of Adam,
cast into great misfortune, as you see.
Yet my heart is still stout -
I don't repent, not in the least,
for killing that fool Abel,
or because of the Father's curse.
Look at me: all overgrown with hair.
I don't dare be seen by any
human being alive,
because I am excommunicated
with my father Adam's curse
and his great wrath.
Because of this I can find no rest
in any place -
I have become the son of curses.
That is why I never dare to come
among people, but always hide myself
in woods and in bushes
living forever like an animal.
My foolishness was so great
and my heart so proud with it:

although I find no happiness
I will not seek mercy from the Father.
I fear every man, lest he should kill me:
but God the Father himself
has set his mark upon me
with his own hand

(shows the mark)

as you may all see.
He spake thus:
that no man shall kill me
on pain of his certain displeasure.
He announced the strictest charge
that he who killed me
shall be requited seven-fold for it.
But despite that promise
I very much suspect
that He intends me no good:
since I'm in distress
I'll go and hide in the bush.

(He hides in the undergrowth)

SERVANT

By your leave, good master,

I see a great beast
crouching in the bush over there.
Of all the animals, 'tis the strangest
sight -
Look, master, there it is!

LAMECH

Make sure, I say, 'tis not a man,
for I cannot see to aim.
Set my arrow sidelong
so I can shoot at it:
Make no doubt, I shall hit it.

SERVANT

Never doubt me; it can't be anything but
a beast,
and very strange 'tis to see.
Now, look, the arrow's set level:
Draw it back to the head,
like the tried and proven archer you are,
who's slain a thousand beasts
and more, by now.

Lamech shoots.

LAMECH

See, the arrow's on its way -
and the beast is hit, for sure!
Yes, it's dying!
Lead me right to it quickly,
so that I can see
what kind of animal it is.

Cain is struck. Blood appears, and he falls.

CAIN (limping and stumbling)

Help, alas! I'm dying!
No longer can I live!
The arrow's gone right through me,
stuck through my ribs!
I'm almost dead -
I've lived in disgrace
and now you see me thus afflicted.

Lamech comes to him.

LAMECH (to servant)

O you villain, what have you done?
Surely, 'tis a man we have killed -
I hear him crying out all the time.

SERVANT

Yes, the beast is crying out -
I see it limping.
'Tis hurt most cruelly:
I beg you, give me its hide
to make me a cloak to wear.
'Tis strangely hairy and ugly -
I'm sure I don't know what kind
of animal it can be,
it looks like some night-bucca to me -
I reckon 'twill turn out so.

LAMECH

(finds and feels Cain, who has fallen down)

Wait! Let me handle it
since I see so little.
What are you? I can't make up my mind
about you;
tell me if you're a man
or some great beast.

CAIN

Bad luck on you, excommunicated one!
I am Cain, son of Adam!
You have killed me:
Your parents curse upon you,
and my own upon you too!

LAMECH

What? You are Cain, son of Adam?
I can't believe that.
You are so disfigured and bent
and overgrown with hair.
Why were you skulking in the bush like that?
This is amazing!
I cannot recognize you as my ancestor
nor any kinsman of mine.

CAIN

From my body you are descended
and from Adam your forefather:
Now are you accursed,
and you and your children
shall be afflicted
seven-fold, believe me.
You see this - God's mark set upon me,
on my temple here.
No one must interfere with me
on any account, when they recognize this.

LAMECH

You understand, I can distinguish very
little -
nothing that counts, I swear.

Tell me why God set this mark
on your forehead.
However hard I peer at you,
I see little of your countenance
or any mark upon your brow.

CAIN

I'll tell you straight:
truly God was angry with me
and gave me his curse
because I slew my brother.
He was Abel, if you want to know:
because of that I feared
I was going to be killed by everyone;
but God granted me, on pain
of his displeasure
that I should not be so -
that whoever should do it
would suffer greatly for it:
and he set his mark here
on the point of my brow as a sign.
And now I am slain by you
O execrated one -
killed by your own hands!

LAMECH

Alas, to see the time

when I have killed you:
if 'tis you, my ancestor Cain.
My servant was to blame:
he told me to shoot
when I couldn't see at all
or very little, believe me.

CAIN

O Lamech, you are an evil fellow -
though I am worse myself.
This was a great vengeance
and just suffering ordained for me -
Alas the time!

LAMECH

But though you are my forefather
I could not recognize you;
I have not seen you for many years,
and you are so disfigured.

CAIN

I am greatly altered
and overgrown with hair.
I live continually in the heat,
the cold and frost, both day and night.
I won't abide seeing mankind at all

but often have the company of beasts.
All this trouble came to me
for killing that oaf Abel:
Trust me, 'tis true.

LAMECH

Why did you kill him
when he was your closest brother?
'Twas an evil deed, that.

CAIN

Because he ordered me about -
and I was his elder brother!
He didn't respect me in the least.
So I became angry
and killed him in a second -
I've no regret for that,
but for that deed I have
the curse of God,
and of my father and mother too.
Though I'm nearly dead
my heart is still proud.
I fear to seek mercy for myself:
I know he's a stern God
and will not forgive me;
nor will I seek his pardon.

I am dying now:
I will not forgive you!
My soul - I know not where 'twill go:
no doubt to hell, where 'twill abide
both winter and summer.

<u>He dies.</u>

LAMECH

O misery, to see this day,
when Cain my ancestor is dead!

<u>(To servant)</u>

You shall be killed for this,
you vile detestable thief -
I'll knock your brains out!

<u>Strikes him with his staff.</u>

SERVANT

O woe! Alas, I'm dead -
my head savagely broken -
Look - in two!

<u>He dies also.</u>

LAMECH

So, I'll get away from here
as best I can.
No use lamenting for him now.

He goes. Hell smokes and thunders. Devils appear.

1ST DEVIL

Cain the outlaw is dead!
Come and bring him to torment,
and Lamech's servant with him.

They approach Cain and the Servant.

2ND DEVIL

Come, O cursed soul:
you slew your brother Abel
who was a righteous man.
In the fire shall you burn,
and so shall this servant, I swear.
Into hell with you, evil-doers!

The Devils carry them to hell, screeching and snarling.

1ST DEVIL

You shall stay with me down below
in this pit, and burn in the fiery heat.
You'll never come out from there,
nor shall any who disobey the Father.

Hell Mouth closes as they vanish inside.

* *

The Death of Adam

ADAM

Seth, my son, come here,
and listen to what I say.
So long have I lived in this world
and am weary of the great labour
which is mine both night and day.
Therefore, if you can, set off
at once to Paradise
to seek the Oil of Mercy.
Your errand shall not be in vain,
no doubt of that.

SETH

Dear father, I do not know the way,
and have never been there.
Sir, I have no idea what direction
to take to look for Paradise.

ADAM

Keep straight on yonder, to the East.
Do not doubt or mistrust
that you will find the way:
'Twill be thus, through my actions there.
You will see my footprints,
made when I came from Paradise,
burnt right into the ground
when the earth was cursed.
And when you come to the place
you will find at the gate an angel
who will answer to your business;
my request shall not be in vain.
Take full note of all
you see there, my son.

SETH

My dear father, I will go there
as soon as I can.
I'll come to you again straightaway

with the answer,

if it be the Father's will above.

<u>Seth follows Adam's tracks to Paradise.</u>

I see the tracks of my father's feet,

which will lead me to Paradise.

This is a miraculous thing:

where he walked, the earth has not thriven.

Through the temptation of the Devil

we have been driven out of Paradise

and had a cruel fall -

by the Father's ordinance

we are fallen into great trouble -

to our misery and woe!

<u>He approaches the Tree of Life in Paradise; a Maiden is in the top with a Child in her arms. The Serpent hangs in the Tree of Knowledge as before. Cain is in Hell, in torment.</u>

SETH

I see the glorious place

and the angel at the gate,

splendid and beautiful to see.

I'll go to greet him humbly.

Angel of God from heaven above,

much joy and happiness to you!
May it please you, I am sent
by Adam my father to you.

CHERUBIM (MICHAEL)

Come near, Seth, and tell me
without more ado, thine errand;
have no fear of anything.

SETH

This is my errand:
to seek the Oil of Mercy.
Thus I have been charged to tell you
by my father, if it be your will.
For he has grown old
and is now weary of the world;
he is so troubled
that he wants nothing
but cries out all the time
for the Oil of Mercy.

CHERUBIM

Come near the gate and look, Seth;
thou shalt see all Paradise.
Look at everything, and say
what strange things thou seest

inside the garden.

SETH

If you desire it
I'll soon take note
of the wonders that are there.

<u>Seth views the Garden, and everything within it.</u>

CHERUBIM

Now tell me, Seth,
what thou seest inside:
keep nothing back.

SETH

Surely I see a tree
with a serpent aloft in it:
it looks dead and dried up.

CHERUBIM

That is the very same tree
from which thy mother and father
did eat the apple of affliction,
forbidden by the word of God
the Highest, with the strictest charge.

And the serpent thou seest
is the very reptile into which
the Devil entered, so to tempt
thy mother Eve.
For God was wrathful
and ordered me
to drive them out of here.
Tell me what else thou seest.

SETH

I see a flourishing tree,
its top most high aloft,
growing even into Heaven;
and its roots run into the ground,
as low as hell, the mighty pit.
And there I see my brother Cain
in great torment and in trouble,
so that he is full of misery.
And in the top of the same tree
I see a sweet maiden sitting,
and a lovely child in her bosom:
so it appears to me.

<u>The angel plucks an apple from the Tree of Life.</u>

CHERUBIM

I will tell thee plainly:
this is truly named the Tree of Life.
I will fetch some of the fruit
and bring a portion to you:
a large apple.

(He breaks it)

Look, here are three kernels
from the apple.
Take them and conceal them
to carry back to thy father.
When his days are over
and he is buried in the ground,
put a kernel into his mouth
and two others likewise in his nostrils.
From those same kernels hereafter
shall grow a tree that shall
without doubt be very fair.
And when it is fully grown
it will be ready
to bear the Oil of Mercy.
After five thousand and five hundred years
are passed, he may then expect
the Oil of Mercy at any time:
also a Saviour, who in truth
will bring him out of perdition.

Tell this to thy father.
Well may he trust it,
for so it is decreed.
Hurry now from here:
My blessing on thee!

SETH

Much thanks to you, Angel of God,
for revealing all this to me.
I will surely report to my father
everything, just as it is:
how great the wonders are.
In the name of God on high
I will now go home
to my father Adam.

He goes back to Adam with the three pips.

Joy to you, my father!
I am now come from Paradise
by the grace of God.
My task is done
just as you ordered me.

ADAM

My welcome to you, Seth.
What is your news?

If you bring the Oil of Mercy
here to your father,
how happy I shall be.

SETH

Truly, not yet, my father.
I'll tell you the truth about everything
as I must.
When five thousand and five hundred years
are fully passed, then
you shall find the Oil of Mercy.
In Paradise I saw
various wonders, believe me:
especially a glorious tree
reaching aloft most strongly to heaven
as I believe: and its roots
reaching low into the ground
even down to hell.
And, no mistaking this, I saw
my brother Cain in torment.
Now in the top of the fair tree
there was a sweet virgin
and her child, most finely wrapped
in her bosom, wondrously to be desired.

ADAM

Glory be to God the Father

for these tidings.
Surely, I have had no joy so great
for more than a hundred years
now past.

SETH

I saw a tree also
with a serpent high in it -
dried up and dead it looked.

ADAM

That indeed was the evil reptile
that deceived your mother Eve.
Thus we lost everything
of the joys of Paradise for ever.

SETH

Here are three pips, brought
to you from Paradise.
They were taken from an apple
which came from the trec
that is named the Tree of Life.
The angel told us
when your days are ended
and you are passed on from here
to put a kernel in your mouth

and the others separately
into your nostrils.
From the kernels there shall grow
a tree, to be most precious
in time to come, and certainly most
beautiful.
When it is full grown
it will then be ready
to bear the Oil of Mercy.

ADAM

Great honour to the Father God
for granting me salvation,
though 'twill be a long time hence.
Hearken to me, Seth my son:
I charge you with my sincere blessing -
make sure you worship the Father of Heaven
and always trust in him
whatever your needs may be.
He will surely help and support you
to a long life in this world.
Head these words of mine, my son.

SETH

Dear father, many thanks to you
for all your good instruction.

Certainly I must worship
the God of the true Trinity,
his excellent Son,
and the Holy Spirit, all three:
since I believe they are One
and Three Persons most worthy,
reigning in bliss in the Kingdom
of Heaven which is above.
Therefore I know I must
worship them with a pure heart.

<u>Death approaches Adam.</u>

ADAM

I have grown old and weak:
I have no more life in me.
Death has come to me:
he will not let me live
here any longer.
I see him with his spear,
ready to pierce me through:
there is no escape for me.
I am eager now the time has come:
I have toiled long in this world
since I was first made.
By my reckoning I am
nine hundred and thirty years old:

'tis time to go hence.
Truly I have had many children
begotten of Eve, my wife:
thirty-two sons have been born
apart from Cain and Abel:
also we have had, since the world began
thirty-two daughters; no word of a lie.
The world has been populated
by me and my children
with numbers uncounted.
This I acknowledge to God with thanks.

DEATH

Adam, be ready for me:
You see I am come with my spear
to take away your life.
Your waiting is at an end:
therefore I shall pierce you
through the heart.

<u>Death strikes him with his spear; he falls.</u>

ADAM

Death, I thank you greatly
for taking my life from this world,
for I am most weary of it;

so I give thanks to God.
I am happy now that for me
the labour and the grief of the world is over:
long have I toiled here,
and so, to the Trinity,
I do commit my soul.

He dies. Devils appear in Hell Mouth.

1ST DEVIL

Comrades and devils, everyone -
Be ready!
The soul of Adam has passed!
Let's go to fetch it down to hell's kitchen
below into the deep pit.

LUCIFER

No! You may not do that:
Other things are decreed for him.
He shall abide there,
in Limbo, at the top:
as the Father ordains.
You know indeed that in hell
there are mansions

where abide the devils
who came out of heaven's light,
bearing great authority with me.
This fellow Adam's resting place
shall be in the upper cloisters
where there shall be no happiness
but great darkness
in the Father's absence.
His son Cain shall have greatest
punishment
and shall remain in direst torment evermore.
He is burning down there
in a deep pit at the bottom.

3RD DEVIL

Why shouldn't the peasant Adam
be tortured in the same way?
Before I rest, I'll get the bastard
a tougher sentence if I can,
since he broke the commandment.

LUCIFER

I'll tell you how it is:
though Adam sinned so greatly
he repented keenly;
so God withheld his displeasure
and his great anger.

But Cain did not do so -
he who killed his brother
felt no repentance at all.
he exulted greatly
and cared nothing for the Father's wrath.
So he shall remain there evermore,
like a dog, in great pain.
The joy of heaven he is denied.
Yes, for Cain and his kind
who would live in the same way,
the place is ordained at the bottom of
hell -
But Limbo is reserved for Adam -
vengeance on him! -
yes, Limbo for him and his sort;
for they shall not suffer the greatest
torment.

1ST DEVIL

Then, by the Great Devil, all our
business
isn't worth an eggshell!
Let the lout stay where he is.
Let's go back to hell, comrades,
to the everlasting torture.

<u>They go back to hell with great noise.</u>

An angel conveys Adam's soul to Limbo.

ANGEL

O soul of goodman Adam,
come with me to hell.
There is a place appointed for thee
by the Father, where thou
shalt remain for a time.
But when the Oil of Mercy comes
you shall be brought to joy
in heaven high above.

SETH

Now that my father is dead
I will bury him.
Let us go hence
and place the body in the earth
with song and solemnity.
From the dust he was made
and to the same dust
he shall surely be returned.
And as I was told to do beforehand,
the three kernels I put into
his mouth and nostrils.

He places the pips in Adam's mouth and nostrils.

He was the first man
to be created by the Father:
behold him now in his grave.
Thanks be to God the Father
for his works here.

The body of Adam is taken to his tomb and laid to rest; choral music is sung.

* *

Enter Enoch.

ENOCH

My name is Enoch,
a faithful servant of the Father.
Truly, I am the son of Jared,
the seventh generation of a great line,
descended from Adam.
Moreover, I am now aged
three hundred and sixty years,
and five more still, if I remember aright.
I pray to the Creator of Heaven
that I shall always willingly
serve him in this world
without fail, whilst I live.

The Father speaks from heaven; Enoch kneels.

THE FATHER

Enoch, I tell thee,
this is my will:
that thou shouldst be straightway
translated.
I will that in body and soul
thou shalt be swiftly brought
to Paradise:
Be ready now at any time.
There thou shalt stay
till the end of the world is nigh;
the secret of this great mystery
I shall not reveal
to anyone at all in the world.

Music. Enoch is carried to Paradise by angels.

ENOCH

May God the Father be glorified!
Thy will be done always!
This is a great and wonderful thing:
I am being taken I know not where.
I faithfully believe and know

that this is God's doing.
I see I have come to Paradise -
A delightful place it is here:
Long in it I shall dwell.
Truly, through the devil's tempting with
   the apple
my forefather Adam has lost
a glorious place indeed:
thus there is misery for all his issue.
Therefore, people of the world,
do not break the laws
which God ordains for you,
for fear of coming to a bad end
with great trouble on all sides.
If you hearken to me
the joys of heaven, in their train
you shall have hereafter.

* *

<u>Enter Seth and Jared.</u>

SETH

There is so much sin in the world

done by men without redress,
that God the Father is angry
that ever he created man.
Destruction for all the world
is most surely ordained:
Everything shall be made void.
This I understand
through the knowledge given to me
by the Father on high.
The planets above and also the stars
are giving plainest signs.

<u>He points to the sun, the moon and the heavens.</u>

The sun and moon as well,
all are moving in conjunction
towards this purpose.
The destruction shall be great,
so that the world shall be overwhelmed
by immense floods of water
or shall be consumed by fire:
believe me if you are wise.
Therefore, let men fear
to offend the Father God
in any way whatever.
In order to avoid that danger,
everything from the world's beginning

is written down by me,
so that everything done in it
shall be truly recorded.

<u>He shows four books.</u>

Behold, here are the books:
as you see, amazingly large.
Everything in the world
is written down in these,
lest they be forgotten.
I will set up two pillars now
for that purpose.
One shall be of brick
and the other of marble.
They shall be made to protect the books.

<u>Seth and Jared build two pillars, one of brick, one of marble.</u>

The brick, so they shall not be burnt by
any fire;
and the marble, in truth, that nothing
shall be destroyed by water:
since it is a tough stone
and wonderfully hard.

JARED

Look, here are the pillars prepared.
Put the books inside them.
Not an art has been forgotten,
nor anything else in truth -
all is written in them.
A copy of every kind of book
is included therein:
Likewise, classifications are planned
in them, by differences and likenesses.
Now I will establish them:
the record shall exist for all time
in very surety in one of these.

<u>They set the pillars upright.</u>

SETH

Therefore, let all the people have fear,
and let us all pray to the Father
that the vengeance shall never fall
on us, or on our children.

* *

Thunder. Heaven opens.

THE FATHER

I now regret that I made man
finely wrought as I myself.
By trusting to a woman
he has completely lost the place
I made for him at my right hand.
When he broke my law
the angel instantly cast them
right out of Paradise.
The spirit shall not abide forever
in any human body in the world,
and the why and wherefore is
that he is made of tender flesh
and with it, very frail.
Now no man serves me faithfully
and truly in all this world
but Noah, and his wife and children too.
Thus is my will:
to exact retribution upon the whole world
so that all shall be destroyed:
though I desire to save certain ones.

Noah and his sons enter.

NOAH

I am Noah, son of Lamech:
a great lord in this world -
remember that, all of you!
I live in plenty with riches and substance,
and therefore must worship my good Lord
the Trinity on High.

THE FATHER (in Heaven)

Noah, come to me now
and hearken to what I say.

NOAH (kneels)

I am ready, excellent Lord:
tell me your will.

THE FATHER (in Heaven)

Noah, the world is now so full of wickedness
that the end is come for all flesh in it.
In very truth they stink with sin.
I can no longer hold back from bringing
death upon everyone except thee,
thy wife and thy children,
and all thy possessions.
Therefore, hasten: go and make
a ship from planks planed down,
with many chambers in it:

rooms they shall be called.
Let it be made watertight with pitch,
inside and outside too.
This vessel shall be a good three hundred
cubits
in length, and thou shalt make its
breadth fifty cubits; 'tis my will
that its height be made thirty.
Abaft thou shalt make a narrow door
called a port. Thou shalt pin beams
through it, so that it shall not open
abroad.
Every manner of species, male and female
both
thou shalt put on board thy ship;
make sure thou bringest every sort of
food
there is, for man and beast as well:
take care 'tis all put aboard thy ship.

NOAH

Mighty lord, I'll do thy bidding, surely;
I'll get moving on the task right away.
I'll cut the pieces of timber with my axe,
freshly sharpened; I'll plane all the
planks

and fix them surely.

<u>Noah and his sons take up tools and timber to make the Ark. They have a beam, a mallet, a caulking iron, ropes, masts, pitch and tar.</u>

SHEM

I'll caulk for you, and do a thorough job,
so no water can get in, even if
it pours down on it;
I promise you that.

HAM

I have pitch, and all sorts of ropes,
and plenty of masts of various kinds.

<u>Music. Time passes: Noah and his sons build the Ark. After a space Tubal Cain enters and watches.</u>

TUBAL CAIN

'Tis an amazing thing to me,
that you should be so simple, Noah.
What's in your mind, to build so grand a vessel
here inland away from the sea?
There isn't a puff of good sense

in going to such expense as this:
all this toil of yours isn't worth a cat!
On my soul, I swear you're an idiot!

<u>He laughs scornfully.</u>

NOAH

My friend, don't be surprised:
you and thousands more will weep for this.
You may laugh now, but not a word of a lie,
You'll see swift retribution in the end.
I have been warned by God the Father
to build this vessel, to save
myself and my children from that very
vengeance.
In a short time you shall see
that all the world will be drowned
by the vastest flood of water.

TUBAL CAIN

Better you were hanged,
you and all your followers,
you scurvy bald-headed old fool!
How d'you make that out -
the world shall be destroyed?
If all the waters of the earth should
come together

they wouldn't finish it off like that.
But all the world can see you're mad.
Vengeance on your scabby head!
Not a man in the land will believe you,
devil a bit!
What's there to worry about?
Does God want to drown the world?
If you know, tell me the reason for it,
in all decency, I beg you.

NOAH

'Tis like this, neighbour:
there is so much sin in the world
and not a sign of improvement,
that God the Father is angered
by all the people of this earth;
He is sorry now that man
was ever created.
Therefore, make amends:
renounce your foolish ways.
Then, if you repent
in the right way
this wrath will be spared.

TUBAL CAIN

Who made you a preacher

to lecture us here?
I pray you, tell me this,
did God speak only to you,
and to nobody else here?
I know of plenty of men
across the country who talk about the
Father;
they're perfect folk, great fellows,
I tell you, who hope for God's favour.
He'd have revealed this flood and
destruction
to some of them, I'm sure.
So I shan't believe you, any more than a
dog.
And we shan't need to behave better,
despite your vain words.

NOAH

You had better be wise,
you and everyone in this world.
Trust me, God will never be found a liar;
be advised by Him.
If you don't, before long
great retribution will fall on you,
for indeed, our Father God will send
a real deluge of water
to drown the world.

With God's help we'll soon build this
ship,
to avoid the danger and save
myself, my wife and children too.

TUBAL CAIN

Fiddlesticks! Cat's fart!
I still don't believe now
that God will do it.
I'm sure he didn't make the world
and everybody in it
to be destroyed so soon.
'Tis impossible to find
all the water to do it!

NOAH

Nothing is impossible
to the Maker of the whole world;
He could even destroy it
inside a single hour.
For by a word everything was made -
heaven and earth, all that is here;
and believe me, if he wishes,
by another word he can destroy it
by a flood.

TUBAL CAIN

It seems to me useless
to argue with you, Noah.
I'll go away, for you're an obstinate mule
who'll never be any good.
A more perfect fool you never saw,
and I'll tell you why:
the vessel was begun a good while ago,
as you recall; more than a score of
years -
and so grandly was it begun,
I swear on my conscience
'twill never be finished!

Exit Tubal Cain.

Music. Time passes. The Ark is completed at last.

NOAH

See now, the ship is built
to my satisfaction, goodly and fair.
Bring every kind of beast to me quickly,
in pairs: cattle, and birds as well,
male and female, two by two.

Music. The sons and their wives and children bring animals and birds to enter the Ark.

SHEM (when all are inside)

There's no beast or reptile in the world,
male and female, I have not brought to you.
Look, there they are in the ship.

Thunder. It begins to rain.

Get ready, father! The flood is coming!
So many men in the world
have said until now
that you were mad to make this ship
here, so far inland
with no sea to bear it away!

JAPHET

They laughed it to scorn:
they had no fear of God's wrath then,
I know that well enough.

NOAH

Now is the flood come -
we had better hurry!
All the animals have gone
into the ship in their kinds,
as it was decreed to me.
Go aboard, my children,

and your wives with you;
the earth is almost covered
by the rain from above.

(To his wife, who is still outside)

You, woman - come on board!
What's this - d'you want to be drowned?

NOAH'S WIFE

We must save what we can;
we mustn't abandon
goods we could keep.
All these things here
cost a lot of money -
you know that, Noah dear.

Noah makes her go aboard.
Music. The Ark sails on the water.

NOAH

'Tis now indeed a long time
since we lost sight of land:
Therefore, go for me, Raven,
Fly off now and see
if land can be found.

I will send the dove as well
to see if she can sight the shore.

Heaven opens.

THE FATHER

Everything which had the spirit of life
within it is now dead.
I will now command
the rain to cease forthwith.

The dove returns with an olive branch in her beak and gives it to Noah.

NOAH

Thanks be to God the Father!
The dove has come back with a green olive branch;
let another one go.
The raven does not wish to return;
she has found some carrion.
'Tis now almost a year
since the Flood began.
If 'tis the purpose of God himself,
the Maker of heaven and earth,
to abate this great flood,
may the will of both Son and Father

be always fulfilled by us here.

<u>The flood subsides.</u>

THE FATHER

Noah, I command thee now
to go forth from thy ship,
thy wife and children also;
animals, birds and all cattle.

NOAH

Great honour to Thee, Lord of Heaven:
thou succourest both weak and strong
most surely, when help is needed.
Let us go forth, great ones and small,
cattle, birds and beasts,
all that were brought on board.
To atone for our sins
I will make an altar:
I will sing hymns
and shall now sacrifice
some of every kind of species,
of birds and animals alike,
to honour Him withall.
And, therefore, let us sing here
in worship to the Father.

All leave the Ark. Choral music.

Before an altar the offerings are made, and incense burnt.

THE FATHER

This is a sweet savour,
and a goodly sacrifice as well.
Verily this pleases me, Noah,
being made to me from a full heart.
Therefore I will cause hereafter
the rainbow to be seen in the sky.

The rainbow appears.

Whenever I see it
I will remember you.
Trust thyself to me:
no more destruction of this sort
will I ever cause this world:
therefore multiply, replenish the earth
with people once more;
all birds and beasts in the world,
and fish in the sea as well
shall be food for you here:
there is nothing in this world
but shall serve you.
Be careful that no human being

shall ever be slain by you:
and if it should be so,
I will require of that man
that his own blood be spilled.
Here in my own image
did I shape the aspect of man:
if you love me, as you ought,
you will hearken to my words.

NOAH

We shall do so, Lord,
as we must indeed,
and shall worship Thee
since 'tis our duty always.

* *

EPILOGUE

Thanks be to God the Father:
on this day which now is over,
you have all seen, high and low,
many matters acted out,
and the creation of the whole world.
Also you have all seen

the same world destroyed
by great floods of water.
Not a man was spared except Noah, his wife
and children.
Come in time tomorrow:
you shall see very great matters,
and redemption granted
by the mercy of God the Father
to save those who are lost.
Minstrels, pipe for us
that we may dance together
as is the manner and the fashion.

Music. Dancing by the whole cast of actors with audience joining them.

THE END

NOTES ON THE TRANSLATION

(Line numbers refer to the Mordon-Caradar version published by the Cornish Language Board.)

Page

17 Lucifer:

'Thou shalt see me rebounding here,

proud and powerful!'

Ty a'm gwel cref omma

Whath pur browt ow trebuchya.

Ow trebuchya seems to mean here 'recoiling' or 'springing back', rather than the weak rendering 'returning'. (M-C, line 269).

30 Eve:

'I will go for a walk'

The verb here is gwandra; translated by M-C as 'ramble'. Other senses given by Nance in his dictionary are 'stroll', 'wander', 'walk about'. (Line 537).

32 Serpent:

'I fear there will be great trouble

if you betray me.'

Saw yma dhym ahanas

dowt pur vras a anfusy

mara qures ow dyskevra.

The full sense is: 'But I have grave fear of misfortune, in case you should expose (betray) me.' Dowt here is clearly fear, not doubt. (Line 573).

33 Eve:

'By St. Michael! My thanks indeed,'

Myghal! Syra, dheugh gromercy,

M-C gives, 'Sir, gramercy to you.' But 'Gramercy' was originally grand merci, 'great thanks'. (Line 598).

34 Eve:

'then truly, by the saints'

Yn urn-na, re Synt Defry,

Not a saint found in the church calendar or any Cornish parish. M-C translates, 'by Saint Verily', which hardly helps. (Line 605).

34 Eve:

'I can't bear to wait any longer.'

Perthy ny allaf pella.

M-C gives, 'I can contain myself no longer.' (*Perthy*: to endure, bear, hold out, etc.) (Line 609).

35 Eve:

'Why do you tempt me like this?'

Prag y whreth genef flattra?

Flattra, an English loan word, still retains in Cornish its sense of 'to wheedle', 'beguile', 'delude', 'talk flowery nonsense'. So M-C is literally correct: 'Why dost thou use cajolery with me?' (Line 634).

39 Serpent:

'You'll thank me for this.'

Ty a yl gothvos dhym gras rag an vyaf.

M-C gives, 'Thou mayst fell grateful to me for the affair.', which is clumsy and unsatisfactory. Literally this is, 'You can know thanks to me for the undertaking.' (Line 713).

39 Eve:

'Now I'll put my best foot forward.'

Kerdhes pur gref my a vyn.

Literally, 'Walk very strongly I will.'

(Line 719).

41 Adam:

'I shall be in trouble if this

was picked from the forbidden tree.'

<u>My a grys, ty, mar pe hemma terrys</u>

<u>mes an wedhen dyfennys</u>

<u>ragtho my a vyth grevyes</u>.

<u>My a grys, ty</u>, is the mediaeval equivalent of 'I believe,you'. M-C uses 'look you', preferring a Welsh expression to a Cornish dialect one. (Line 752).

58 'Dung': What Cain is referring to is dried cow-dung, used for fuel. (Cornish <u>Glosen</u>, collective <u>glos</u>). Burn easily: <u>hep bern</u>: without regret or care; i.e. something expendable. (Line 1090)

61 Cain:

'He's old and experienced enough
now'

<u>Coth yu ef hag aflythys</u>:

Literally, 'of age he is and hardened', i.e. experienced. (Line 1150).

63 Cain:

'I reckon he's worse than a bucca:'

My a'n syns gweth es bucca:

'I hold him (to be) worse than a hobgoblin:' Buccas, however, could be beneficial, especially in the mines; hence 'evil bucca'. M-C translates bucca as 'imp'. (Line 1194).

65 Adam:

'Because the child we loved the most is dead'

dre vernans ow flogh nep a garen an moyha

'through the death of my child whom I loved the most' (M-C, lines 1228-9).

65 Adam:

'Bear up!'

Na sor!

M-C, 'Do not give way!'. Literally, 'Do not be vexed', 'agitated'. (Verb. serry). (Line 1245).

66 Adam:

'The wrath of God increases ...'

Sor Dew, ha trobel pup tu, yma pup owr ow cressya.

'God's wrath, with trouble on all sides, is every hour increasing.' (M-C, lines 1254-5).

71 Cain:

'I dare not be seen'

rag ny bejyaf bos gwelys:

Literally, 'I won't (can't) bear to be seen.' (Verb. pejya or pesya.) (Line 1669).

75 Lamech:

'they're not fastidious -'

nyns yns denty -

M-C: 'they are not particular' - i.e. they don't worry about things. (Line 1454).

86 Lamech:

'I'll knock your brains out!'

Squattyes yu dha ympynyon:

'Shattered are your brains'. A future

sense is intended, since this precedes the stage direction. (Line 1700).

96 Seth:

'... wondrously to be desired.'

wondrys whans.

M-C: 'wondrously to be longed for.' (whans, as adjective, does not appear in Nance's dictionary). (Line 1910).

111 The Father:

'... the place
I made for him at my right hand.'

An plas a'm luf dhyghow a wrussen.

M-C: 'The place which by my right hand I had made' is ambiguous. (Line 2215).

113 Noah:

'I'll get moving on the task right away.'

Ow lythyow hep falladow
My a vyn dalleth stretchya.

Literally, 'My limbs without fail I will begin to stretch.' (Line 2281)

125 The Father:

'and if it should be so,
I will require of that man
that his own blood be spilled.'

<u>ha mar pedha yndella</u>
<u>my a vyn y requyra</u>
<u>an dhywla a'n keth den-ma</u>
<u>y wos a dheff' ha scullys.</u>

The sense is involved and difficult; literally,

'and if it should be so,
I will require it of the hands
of that same man (that) his blood
should come to spill.

(Lines 2520-3).

Notes on

THE PRODUCTION OF THE CREATION PLAY

mediaeval and modern.

All productions of the Cornish miracle plays must to a great extent be based on the conditions imposed by the mediaeval open-air Round, or Plain-an-Gwarry, whatever their actual circumstances: whether indoors, in hall or theatre, in churches, or out of doors. The Cornish plays were certainly all composed for presentation in the rounds of Cornwall, which were generally, but not always, Iron Age fortifications once lived in or used as refuges by the Celtic inhabitants up to the 6th or 7th centuries A.D. Piran Round near Perranporth, and Castilly near Lanivet are the best extant examples. Professor Charles Thomas of the Institute of Cornish Studies and other archaeologists believe they have located some thirty such Plain-an-Gwarry; Castilly and Piran Round in particular bears evidence of the terracing of the original banks for audiences to sit on. In some cases, however, as at St. Just in Penwith, Plain-an-Gwarry at Redruth and Playing Place near Truro, and almost certainly at Glasney in Penryn, the 'theatres' were suitable open spaces adapted to this use, being near to the congregations for whom the productions were intended.

In the Rounds God and Heaven were always placed on the east; Hell at the North entrance. (Hell Mouth was usually in the form of a huge dragon's head with moveable jaws that could open to admit or expel the devils (see the stage direction on p.16 - 'Hell Mouth opens wide ...'). Worldly potentates (emperors, kings, etc.) would be on the west, opposite Heaven: and great Christian figures, popes and patriarchs, on the south. Evidence for this survives, particularly in the manuscript of Bewnans Meriasek (Peniarth MS 105, a copy of which is in the Royal Institution of Cornwall, Truro) which contains a plan of the play, deploying the various stations in exactly that way. Professor Richard Southern's book, 'Mediaeval Theatre', explores this matter and proposes a very satisfactory scheme of 'towers' or 'pavilions' from whence these personages descend to enact their scenes, retiring up again at their conclusions. Thus the numerous Ordinalia directions descendit and ascendit are explained; also, in the Creation, such passages as God's command: 'Michael, bright angel, descend ...'. In modern Cornwall this arrangement has been adopted by producers of the Ordinalia, Creation, etc., with complete success. The stations as used for the 1973 production at Piran Round are shown on p.136.

One vital piece of stage machinery still exists at Piran: the conveyor. A spoon-shaped depression in the ground reaches out from below Heaven almost into the centre of the arena (which is 150 feet in diameter). This was evidently covered, either with some stuff or material, or wicker-work with grass, leaves, etc. on it; so that at the right moment in the play Adam and Eve suddenly appeared and were created in the centre. Whether they could originally enter the conveyor from outside the earth banks, or had to be installed beforehand inside the shallow tunnel, is a question we must leave archaeologists to resolve. The stage direction in the original is clear enough: 'Adam and Eve, apparelled in white leather, in a place appointed by the conveyor, and not to be seen till they be called, and they kneel and rise'. In the 1973 production Adam and Eve, clad in white body stockings (in lieu of suits of white leather) lay concealed in the bowl of the 'spoon' until God the Father raised them up for all to see.

Some other technical problems of 1973 and their solutions may be of interest. The battle of the Angels was conducted, not with swords, but with seven-feet long oak staves, the actual war being a series of intricately worked-out cudgel fights in groups all over the arena. The transformation of Lucifer into the Serpent, an obvious teaser, was effected thus: a girl actor appeared in the Serpent's costume, a blue-green shiny material with a hood and long trailing tail to it, and performed a sinuous dance to music. Following this (p.30) Lucifer engaged and 'wrestled' with her, in so doing wrapping the cloak and hood around himself - at which the actress fled the scene.

The Devils wore horrific masks, specially made to fit their faces, which they put on in Hell after being overcome and dragged there by the victorious angels. Other features such as black winged costumes, humps, horns, limps, tails and claws were all assumed under the shelter of the sixteen-feet high skull which represented the infernal regions: a huge black cape being hung beneath its jaws, from under which at times smoke belched. The appearance of the Devils (e.g. to pounce on the dead Cain, and to attempt to take Adam's body) were punctuated with the detonation of maroons.

The Garden of Eden was a trellised enclosure near the centre, dressed out with flowers and vegetation, with the Trees of Life and Knowledge clearly visible within it. The

Rainbow was an arch constructed on the principle of a fan, with gauze material stretched over it, raised over the South gate at the appropriate moment (p.124). The Ark was a skeleton ship, brought in piece by piece into the arena by Noah's sons, in which all the persons and animals sat: masks again being worn by the latter, who were mainly children from Perranporth School. The effect of the flood was created by rowing actions, music, and lighting. Incidental music and effects were provided by a 20-strong band from Newquay School, playing under an awning situated on the perimeter of the arena, between Heaven and Hell.

A few remarks on interpretations. Lucifer, the first to set himself up against God, was certainly seen by the director as the prototype rebel or revolutionary. God became at times a figure of fun, petulantly baffled by his creation which was clearly getting out of hand. Eve, a complex and at times infuriating character, carries the revolt process a step farther, though entirely without realising what she is doing. (She, like Lucifer, covets the omniscience and omnipotence of the Father, but much as an inquiring child might.) Cain, too, is an interesting character, the third (if Adam be excepted - he was clearly blackmailed by Eve) to rebel: the first to find a convincing reason for his disobedience, and to have faith in his own pride - a mortal sin, it must be remembered. One cannot help sympathising with Cain: the anonymous writer of his scenes probably should have been excommunicated. As the play moves on man becomes more and more alienated from God, and to emphasize this aspect an effective scene, played to some very sophisticated sleazy music, was interpolated just before the Flood, and entitled the Dance of the Seven Deadly Sins. The final reconciliation between Noah, representing humanity, and a rather chastened Father who had now himself grown up through his experiences, was all the more moving as a result.

